Robert Pęczko

Colour illustrations by
Zygmunt Szeremeta

Mitsubishi
J2M Raiden

STRATUS

Published in Poland in 2004 by STRATUS
Artur Juszczak, Po. Box 123, 27-600 Sandomierz 1, Poland
e-mail: arturj@mmpbooks.biz
for
Mushroom Model Publications,
36 Ver Road, Redbourn,
AL3 7PE, UK.
e-mail: rogerw@waitrose.com

© 2004 Mushroom Model Publications.
http://www.mmpbooks.biz

ISBN 83-916327-7-6

Editor in chief	Roger Wallsgrove
Editors	Bartłomiej Belcarz
	Robert Pęczkowski
	Artur Juszczak
Edited by	Robert Pęczkowski
Page design by	Artur Juszczak
	Robert Pęczkowski
Cover Layout	Artur Juszczak
DTP	Robert Pęczkowski
	Artur Juszczak
Translation	Wojtek Matusiak
Proofreading	Roger Wallsgrove
Colour Drawings	Zygmunt Szeremeta
Scale plans	Mariusz Kubryn

Printed by: Drukarnia Diecezjalna, ul. Żeromskiego 4, 27-600 Sandomierz
tel. (15) 832 31 92; fax (15) 832 77 87
www.wds.pl   marketing@wds.pl

WYPRODUKOWANO W POLSCE
PRINTED IN POLAND

On the title page: J2M3 (S-12) captured and evaluated by the Americans in 1945.

via A. Lochte

Table of contents

Acknowledgements:

The author would like to thank Artur Lochte for providing photos and James F. Lansdale, Jim Long nad Tadeusz Januszewski for their help in the research.

Development

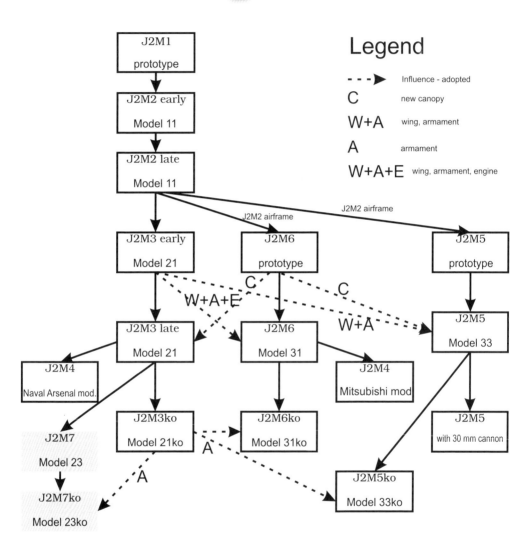

Introduction

The Raiden was designed against a requirement for a high speed and high rate-of-climb land-based interceptor fighter. The specification, novel for the Japanese naval air force, was defined in the late 1930s. The aeroplane was going to be employed for air defence of important strategic positions. This class of aircraft was known in Japan as the Kyôkuchi Sentoki, or Kyôkusen in short. Although normally in Japan a competition for a new aeroplane project should be held, work on this subject was entrusted directly to the Mitsubishi company, and in 1938 the team headed by Jiro Horikoshi commenced work on it. Due to priority of the A6M Zero, preliminary designs for the new aeroplane were not completed before September 1939. Work on the project started in March 1940 under J. Horikoshi, who was assisted by Yoshitoshi Sone and Kiro Takahashi. The project was very innovative by Japanese standards, featuring a low wing with symmetrical airfoil and slotted flaps. In order to minimise drag a very low cockpit canopy was used. Power plant consisted

J2M Raiden prototype - 14Shi side view. 1/72 scale

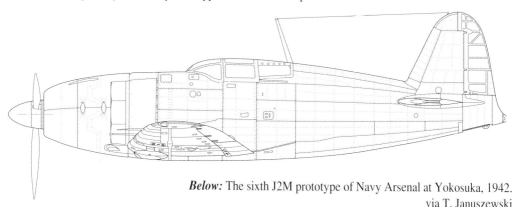

Below: The sixth J2M prototype of Navy Arsenal at Yokosuka, 1942.
via T. Januszewski

Above:
The sixth J2M prototype sent to 302 Kókútai for evaluation.

via T. Januszewski

Above:
Details of the first version of the canopy as used on the first prototype.

via T. Januszewski

Right:
Front view of the one of the J2M prototypes. Note the three blade propeller and early style exhaust.

via T. Januszewski

of one 1,460 hp Mitsubishi Kasei (MK4) radial. The engine cowling was very slim, with a small air intake, which forced the designers to use a fan to achieve proper cooling airflow.

All these innovations resulted in serious delays in work on the prototype. Moreover, Horikoshi concentrated entirely on A6M Zero development, naming Kiro Takahashi as the new leading designer, but remaining in overall control of the project. The aeroplane received the company designation M-20, and the military name of "Naval 14 Shi experimental interceptor fighter" (J2M1).

Construction of the prototype was finally completed in March 1942, and the first flight from Kagamigaura aerodrome took place on 20 May 1942.

A total of 8 development prototypes was built.

J2M2 Raiden Model 11

The first production version, first flown in October 1942.

The main difference with respect to the prototype was the redesigned cockpit glazing, with a flat windscreen panel, and significantly raised. The Kasei 23ko (MK4RF) engine was replaced with one that featured improved cooling and individual exhausts. This engine was also fitted for water/methanol injection. The fan shaft length was reduced to eliminate vibrations. The new engine and shorter shaft resulted in a smaller overall length of the aeroplane.

This version entered production as the "Naval interceptor fighter Raiden Model 11" (J2M2 Raiden Model 11).

Below:
J2M2 Model 11, probably the 20th aircraft in the series.
Bottom:
Raiden Model 11 of Genzan Kókútai. Note the bulge on the wing, the cannon fairing.
photos via T. Januszewski

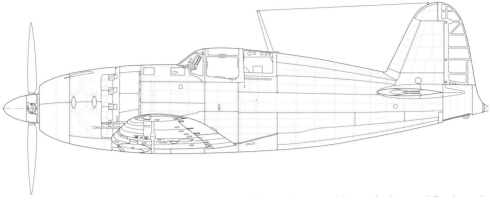

During production this version was subject to further modifications. In order to cure the problems of the engine emitting smoke at maximum power output, the mixture injection angle was changed. Engine vibrations were also a serious problem, and it was attempted to cure this by fitting the engine with shock-absorbers and introduction of propeller blades wider at the base. The fuel tanks were also redesigned and repositioned.

During production an oil cooler air intake was added under the engine.

A total of 131 of these aircraft was built (including prototype no. 4 that formed the pattern for production aircraft). Airframes of this version were also used as basis for new project trials.

Above:
Side view of the early J2M2 without oil cooler intake. 1/72 scale.

Right:
J2M2 (YoD-1171) of 302 Kókútai, 1944.
                via T. Januszewski

Below:
Side view of the late J2M2 Raiden 11.

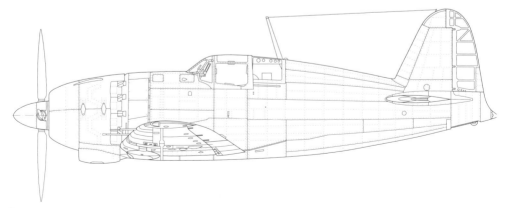

J2M3 Raiden Model 21

Production of this version was started while the J2M2 was still being manufactured. The principal difference lay in the altered armament. The fuselage-mounted machine guns were abandoned in favour of two more cannon in the wings. Thus the aeroplane was armed with two 20mm Type 99 Model 1 and two 20mm Type 99 Model 2 cannon. Fitting of the additional cannon necessitated strengthening of the wing structure. With the machine guns removed, the instrument panel was redesigned. Armour protection was also improved. The changes resulted in increased weight and, consequently, deterioration in the performance of the aeroplane.

After tests of the new J2M6 cockpit canopy proved favourable, this new version started to be fitted in the J2M3, too.

Left:
Two J2M3 in the flight. Aircraft tested by ATAIU S.E.A. just after the war. See colour profile at page 72. "Fanny's Frolic name on the BI-02.

via A. Lochte

Below:
Probably the first prototype of J2M3 Model 21.

via T. Januszewski

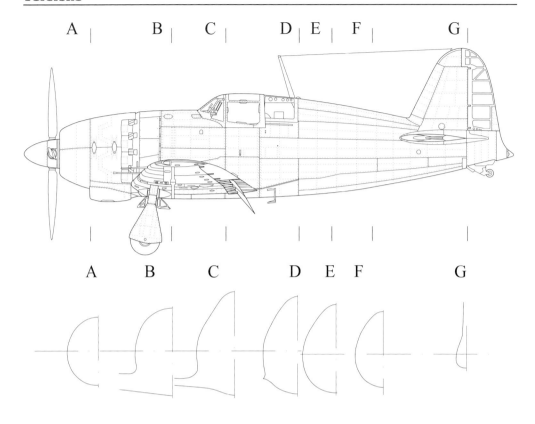

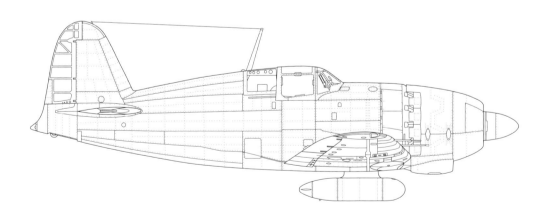

J2M3 Raiden Model 21 1/72 scale plans.

Plan view of the J2M3 Model 21.
1/72 scale.

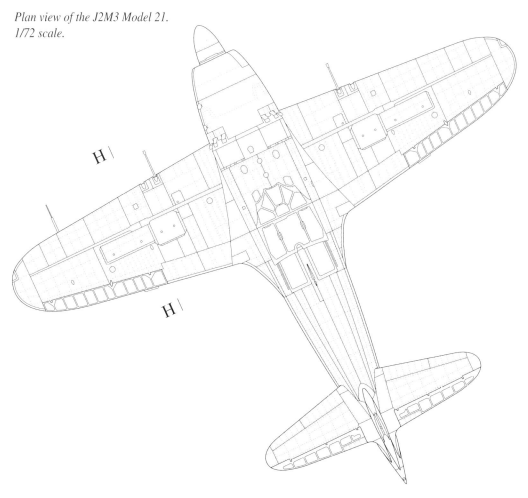

H |

H |

J2M3 Model 21 photo-
graphed just after the
war.

via A. Lochte

J2M3ko Model 21ko

This variant was developed by replacing two wing-mounted Type 99
Model 1 cannon with Type 99 Model 2 cannon in under-wing pods.
21 were built.

A total of some 307 J2M3 aircraft were built by Mitsubishi, and some
128 by the Koza plant.

*Front view of the J2M3
Model 21.
1/72 scale.*

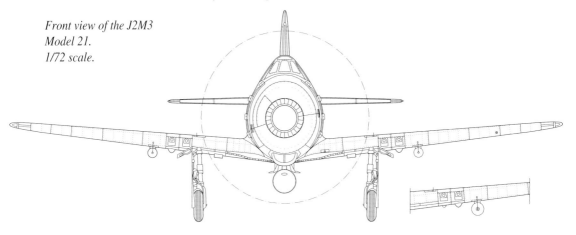

H

*J2M3 "S-12", tested by T.A.I.U - S.W.P.A. in 1945.
via A. Lochte*

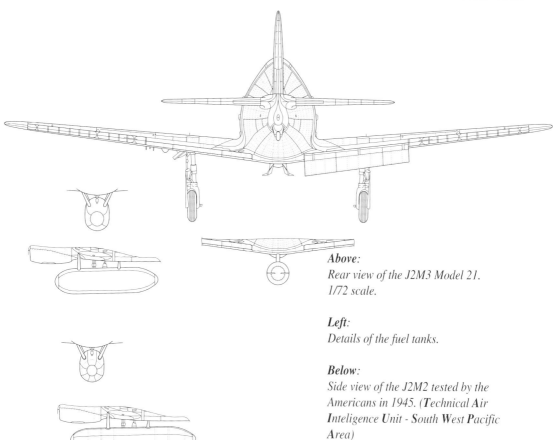

Above:
Rear view of the J2M3 Model 21.
1/72 scale.

Left:
Details of the fuel tanks.

Below:
Side view of the J2M2 tested by the
Americans in 1945. (**T**echnical **A**ir
Inteligence **U**nit - **S**outh **W**est **P**acific
Area)

via A. Lochte

J2M3 Model 21 - undersurface.
1/72 scale plan.

Below:
J2M3 Model 21 "B1-02" being evaluated by
the British in Malaya, 1945.

via A. Lochte

*J2M3 Model 21 of Genzan Kókútai. Air-
craft with 300l drop tank.*

via A. Lochte

Right:
*J2M3 Model 21 "352-20" of
352 Kókútai in 1945.*
via T. Januszewski

*The same aircraft as seen in the top photo,
this time from the side.*

J2M3 Model 21 captured by
the Americans.
via T. Januszewski

Another photo of the Raiden
Model 21 prototype.
Note the landing flap in
down position.
via T. Januszewski

J2M3 Raiden Model 21 of
Tainan Kókútai.
via T. Januszewski

J2M4 Raiden Model 32

Attempts to improve the Raiden's performance focused on turbo-supercharged engine trials. The first prototype of this version was powered by the Mitsubishi Kasei 23hei (Kasei 23a) engine fitted with the same company's supercharger. The prototype used the J2M6 fuselage with two cannon fitted aft of the cockpit. The cannon were going to fire upwards, at around 30 degrees. This version was going to be used against the B-29s that operated at altitudes beyond reach of other Japanese aircraft.

The second prototype of this version was fitted with the same type of engine, but with a different supercharger, made by Dai-Nijuichi Kaigun Kokuso (21st Aircraft Arsenal of the Navy) at Sasebo. This prototype was longer than its predecessor, and featured altered engine cooling gills. The second prototype was designated J2M4Kai Model 32 Kai. This conversion was performed by Yokosuka Kaigun Koku Gijitsusho.

J2M4 with supercharger produced by Dai-Nijuichi Kaigun Kokuso

Only the two prototypes were built because major problems with turbo-superchargers made immediate start-up of series production impossible. American documents listed only one J2M4 aeroplane, describing the other as a J2M3 converted to a supercharged version.

1/72 scale plans.

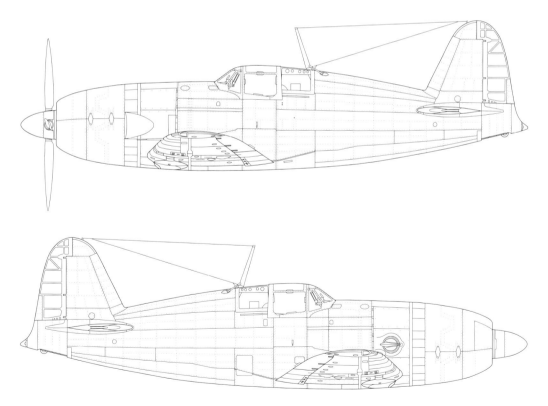

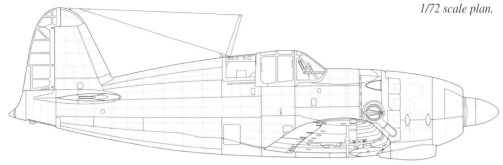

J2M4 with Mistubishi supercharger.
1/72 scale plan.

Photo of the late airframe (J2M3 or J2M6) with Mitsubishi turbocharger. Aircraft "YoD-191" of 302 Kókútai
via T. Januszewski

Another photo of the late airframe (J2M3 or J2M6) with Mitsubishi turbocharger.
It was, probably, a field modification, because the are no records in the official documents about a third J2M4 aircraft.
via T. Januszewski

J2M5 Raiden Model 33

The next version was also going to be a high altitude fighter. The new power plant was tested in J2M2 airframes nos. 42 and 48, fitted with the Kasei 26 engine.

It is not possible to tell whether the new cockpit that featured in production aircraft, and the additional flat profile of the upper fuselage in front of the windscreen, was first used in this version or in the J2M6 developed in parallel. The production version was powered with the Mitsubishi Kasei 26ko engine fitted with a three-stage centrifugal supercharger. This was the fastest Raiden version, reaching a top speed of 615 km/h at 6,800 m.

Mitsubishi plants built some 43 aircraft of this version.

At least one of the aeroplanes, as shown in surviving photos, was armed with two 30 mm Type 5 cannon instead of four 20 mm ones.

It is not impossible that, due to the small number of Kasei 26 engines made, some J2M5 airframes were fitted with Kasei 23ko engines, making them similar to the J2M6.

J2M5 Raiden Model 33 side view. Aircraft with 30mm cannon in the wings 1/72 scale plan.

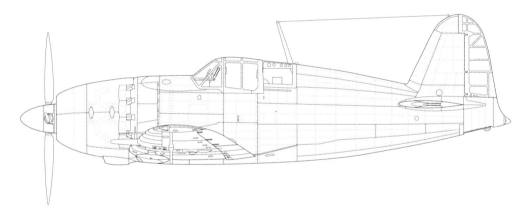

One of the very rare photos of J2M5 Model 33. via T. Januszewski

J2M6 Model 31

Externally this version looked like a combination of the J2M3 airframe with the J2M5 cockpit. Tests of this version were probably carried out using the J2M2 airframe no. 31. It seems very likely that this J2M6 prototype was used for testing of the new cockpit and the flat fuselage top portion in front of the windscreen. Probably two prototypes were built, one being converted to the high altitude version (J2M4). This aeroplane appeared before the J2M4 and J2M5, but development work continued in parallel.

Side view of J2M6 Raiden Model 31.
1/72 scale plan.

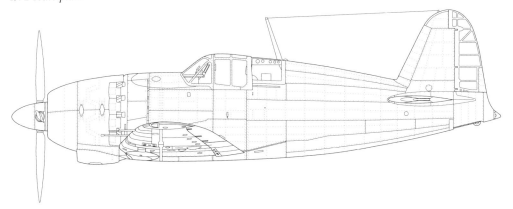

J2M6 Raiden Model 31 of 352 Kokutai or more likely J2M5 airframe with Kasei 23 engine.

via T. Januszewski

Development work and field modifications

The J2M6ko Model 31ko version under development was going to use the J2M3ko airframe with the J2M3 cockpit (similar to the J2M6).

Also the J2M7 model 23 version was under development. The airframe, similar to that of the J2M3, was going to be powered by the Kasei 26ko engine.

Probably several aircraft were used for testing of various supercharged engines.

Other variants were developed:
J2M5ko Model 33ko – Kasei 26ko engine and four 20 mm Type 99 Model 2 cannon,
J2M7ko Model 23ko – ditto.
J2M8 – featuring cut down rear fuselage (all-round vision canopy similar to that of the A6M Zero).

The aeroplane was also subject to modifications by operational units, on individual aircraft.
Many J2M3 aircraft had cannon fitted aft of the cockpit, similar to the J2M4. Unfortunately, the exact number of such modifications is not known.
Also, photographs exist of aircraft with a cannon fitted obliquely under the cockpit and firing upwards.

A line of J2M3 Raidens captured by the Americans.
via T. Januszewski

TECHNICAL DATA

	J2M1 (M-20)	J2M2 Model 11	J2M3 Model 21	J2M4 Model 32	J2M4 Naval Arsenal mod.	J2M5 Model 33	J2M6 Model 31
Wing span [m]	10.8	10.8	10.8	10.8	10.8	10.8	10.8
Length [m]	9.9	9.695	9.695	10.145	9.695	9.695	9.695
Height [m]	3.820	3.875	3.945	3.875	3.875	3.875	3.875
Wing area [m²]	20.05	20.05	20.05	20.05	20.05	20.05	20.05
Empty weight [kg]	2,191	2,348	2,490	2,574	2,823	2,539	2,853
Take-off weight [kg]	-	3,650	4,095	3,946	4,207	3,507	3,947
Wing loading [kg/m²]	142.69	160.1	171.57	171.32	196.86	174.91	173.66
Power loading [kg/kW]	2.71	2.42☐	2.57	2.57	2.95	2.65	2.62
Capacity of							
The main fuel tank [l]	710	420	390	390	390	390	390
Wing fuel tanks [l]	none	none	180	180	180	180	180
Water/methanol mixture tank [l]	none	130	120	120	120	120	120
Oil tank [l]	60	60	60	60	60	60	60
Armament							
Machine guns	two 0.303 in. Type 97	two 0.303 in. Type 97					
Cannon	two 20 mm Type 99 Model 1 Type 3	two 20 mm Type 99 Model 1 Type 4	two 20 mm Type 99 Model 1 two 20 mm Type 99 Model 2	four 20 mm Type 99 Model 1 two 20 mm Type 99 Model 2	four 20 mm Type 99 Model 1	two 20 mm Type 99 Model 1 two 20 mm Type 99 Model 2	two 20 mm Type 99 Model 1 two 20 mm Type 99 Model 2
Bombs	2 x 30 kg	2 x 30 kg	2 x 60 kg	2 x 60 kg	2 x 60 kg	2 x 60 kg	2 x 60 kg
Engine	HA-32-13 (MK4C)	HA-32-23 (MK4RF)	HA-32-23 (MK4RF)	HA-32 -23	HA-32-23hei	HA-32-26	HA-32-23
Take-off rating [kW (hp)]	1,050 (1,430)	1,330 (1,800)	1,340 (1,820)	1,340 (1,820)	1,340 (1,820)	1,330 (1,800)	1,330 (1,800)
Power rating [kW] at altitude [m]	1,030 2,700	1,160 1,800	1,180 1,300			1,110 2,800	1,160 1,800
Power rating [kW] at altitude [m]	930 6,500	1,040 4,800	1,120 4,100	1,040 9,200	1,040 9,200	710 7,200	1,040 2,450
Engine revs [rpm]	2,350	2,450	2,500	2,500	2,500	2,500	2,450
Propeller type	VDM	VDM	VDM	VDM	VDM	VDM	VDM
Diameter [mm]	3,200	3,300	3,300	3,300	3,300	3,300	3,300
Max. speed [km/h] at altitude [m]	578 6,000	596 5,450	612 6,000	577 9,300	577 9,300	615 6,585	590 5,450
Time to climb to altitude [m]		5'38'' 6,000	5'40'' 6,000	19'30'' 10,000	19'30'' 10,000	6'20'' 6,000	5'38'' 6,000
Ceiling [m]	11,000	11,680	11,520	11,500	11,500	11,250	11,520
Range [km]		1,055	1,055	1,110 + 0.5h	1,110+0.5h	555+0.5h	1,055

Mitsubishi and Koza J2M production in 1942-1945.

(all figure totals from USSBS Studies, Pacific War, Report 16 & Report 34)
via James F. Lansdale

Version month/year	J2M1 (14S)	J2M2 (14SK) (Model 11)	J2M3 Model 21	J2M5	J2M6	J2M4
02/1942	1					
03/1942						
04/1942	1					
05/1942	1					
06/1942	1	1 (prototype no 4)				
07/1942	2					
08/1942	1					
09/1942	1					
10/1942		1				
11/1942		1				
12/1942		2				
01/1943						
02/1943						
03/1943		1				
04/1943		2				
05/1943						
06/1943		3				
07/1943		4				
08/1943		5				
09/1943		16				
10/1943		15	1			
11/1943		21				
12/1943		22				
01/1944		17				
02/1944		20 (aprox.)	6 (aprox.)			
03/1944			9			
04/1944			22			
05/1944			38 + 1(K)	1		
06/1944			43		1	
07/1944			34			
08/1944			21 + 1(K)			1
09/1944			16 + 2(K)			
10/1944			20 + 3(K)			
11/1944			18 + 4(K)			
12/1944			7 + 6(K)			
01/1945			17 + 13 (K)			

02/1945			11 + 8 (K)		1	
03/1945			29 + 23 (K)			
04/1945			16 + 15 (K)			
05/1945			10(K)			
06/1945			20(K)	8		
07/1945			22(K)	7		
08/1945				27		
Total	8	131 (aprox.)	307 + 128(K)	43	2	1 + 1 J2M3 converteted to J2M4*

(K) – produced by Koza Kaigun Kokusho

*- 1 J2M3 modified by Yokosuka Kaigun Koku Gijitsusho for J2M4 development

Serials:

Mitsubishi

J2M1 – 201, 302, 403, 504, 605, 706, 807, 908, 209

J2M2 – 2001-2130 (prox.)

J2M3 – 3001-3308 (aprox.)

J2M4 – serials unknown

J2M5 – 15001-15043 (?)   *This photo is very hard to identify. It might to be J2M5 or*

J2M6 – serials unknown   *J2M6 or even J2M5 with Kasei 23 engine.*

Koza   *Simply - new airframe with an old engine.*

J2M3 – 13001-13128 (probably)   *via T. Januszewski*

CODE LETTERS

Unit	Code letters	Code colour	In combat
Kókútai 301	ƎC (YoC) 01	Black White	February 1944 – July 1945
Kókútai 381	81	White	end of 1943 – April 1945
Kókútai 302	ƎD (YoD)	White	March 1944 – August 1945
Kókútai 332	32	White	August 1944 - August 1945
Kókútai 352	3 52	White	August 1944 - August 1945
Kókútai 256	🔲 (Rai)	Yellow	November 1944 – December 1945
Kókútai 1001	01	White	
Kókútai 1081	81	White	From time to time several of Raidens
Yokosuka Kókútai	Ǝ (Yo)	White	From time to time several of Raidens
Yatabe Kókútai	ヤ (Ya)	White	From time to time several of Raidens
Genzan Kókútai (II)	ケ (Ke)	White	From time to time several of Raidens
Tainan Kókútai (II)	タイ (TaI)	White	From time to time several of Raidens
Kónoike Kókútai	コウ (KoU)	White	From time to time several of Raidens
Chúshi Kókútai	コ (Naka)	Red	From time to time several of Raidens

Another photo of the aircraft with the new cockpit.
J2M5 or J2M6.

via T. Januszewski

American Intelligence Identification Card of the Raiden.

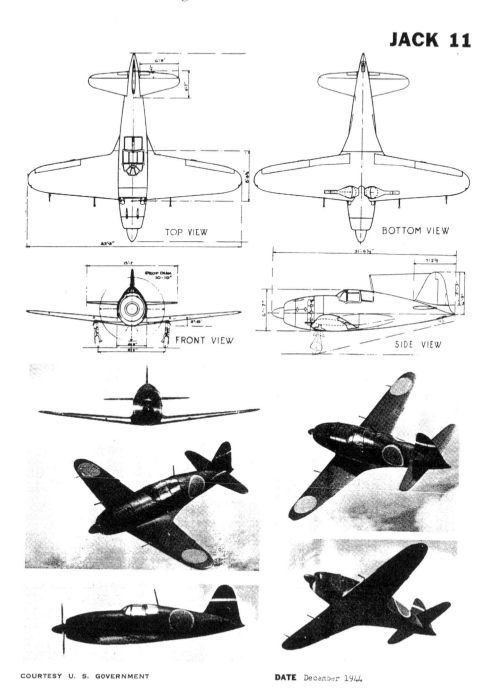

COURTESY U. S. GOVERNMENT   **DATE** December 1944

American Intelligence Identification Card of the Raiden.

JACK 11

FIELDS OF FIRE

FORWARD GUNS
"A", AND "B"
¾-front view from above

EXHAUST FLAME PATTERNS

REAR VIEW

VULNERABILITY

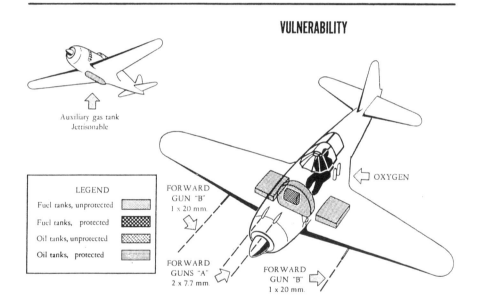

Auxiliary gas tank
Jettisonable

LEGEND	
Fuel tanks, unprotected	▨
Fuel tanks, protected	▨
Oil tanks, unprotected	▨
Oil tanks, protected	▨

OXYGEN

FORWARD
GUN "B"
1 x 20 mm.

FORWARD
GUNS "A"
2 x 7.7 mm.

FORWARD
GUN "B"
1 x 20 mm.

ARMAMENT

	No.	Size	Rds. Gun.	Type		No.	Size	Rds. Gun	Type
Forward	4	20 mm	100	Fixed	Tail				
or	2	7.7mm	550	Fixed					
Top and	2	20 mm	100	Fixed	Wing				
Side									
Bottom									

DATE December 1944

TACTICAL DATA

JACK is more powerful and
heavily armed than previous
Japanese fighters. Probably
less maneuverable than ZEKE
but superior in diving and
climbing at high speeds.

No armor or fuel protec-
tion have been indicated.

COURTESY U. S. GOVERNMENT

FUSELAGE

Above:
An excellent picture of the J2M3 in flight. The fuselage shape is well illusrated, with all panel lines (aircraft is not painted).

> *via A. Lochte*

Right:
Side view of the only J2M3 preserved after the war. Aircraft before restoration.

All photos of preserved J2M3 by A. Lochte (except where stated)

3/4 front view of the Raiden. In this picture aircraft is beautifully restored.

The cockpit section of the J2M3 fuselage, from the left.

Front view of the Raiden. Aircraft without main undercarriage leg covers.

Bottom, mid section of the rear part of the fuselage. Note the shape of the fuselage.

Front, portside part of the fuselage.

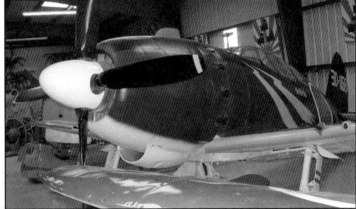

The center section of the fuselage. Note that wing and disassembled aileron is visible.

Above: The forward part of the fuselage from the rear awaiting final assembling. Note the shape of the cross-section.
Left: Portside part of the fuselage just below the cockpit.
Left, below: The handgrip, just below the cockpit.
Below: Access panels on the portside of the fuselage below the aft part of the cockpit.

Above:
J2M3 Raiden Model 21 of
302 Kokutai, during take
off. Note the shape of the
fuselage and undercarriage
arrangement.

via A. Lochte

Right:
Another Raiden during take
off.

via T. Januszewski

J2M3 captured by the
Americans at Atsugi.

via A. Lochte

WING

Top of the starboard wing, inboard section.

Starboard wing with aileron raised.

Ammunition compartment access panel and gun compartments access panels with rotating locks

Above:
The rotating lock to gun
compartment access panel.
Right.
The access panel to gun
compartment.

*The starboard wing looking
aft.*

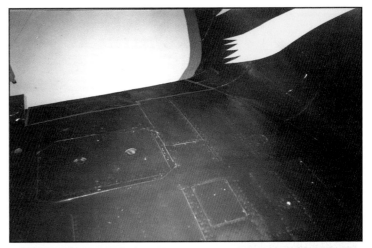

*The starboard wing looking
forward.*

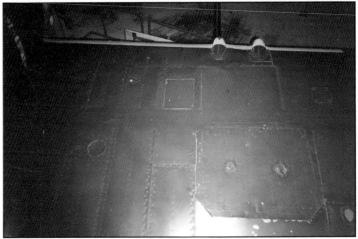

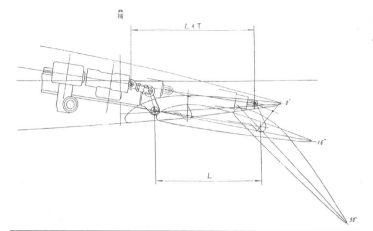

Drawing of the landing flap operating mechanism. Drawing from the Technical Manual.

The starboard, middle part of the wing, looking aft.

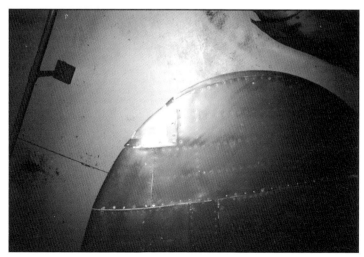

Left:
The starboard wingtip. Position lamp is clearly visible.
Below:
The aileron control cover on the port wing.

Two photos of the gun and ammuniton compartment access panels, with panels removed (**right**) and with all panels in place (**below**).

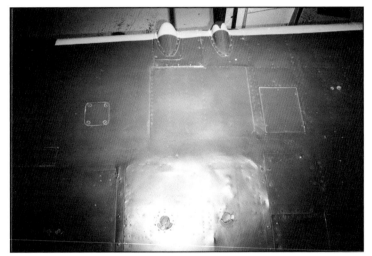

Top of the starboard wing, the aileron control cover.

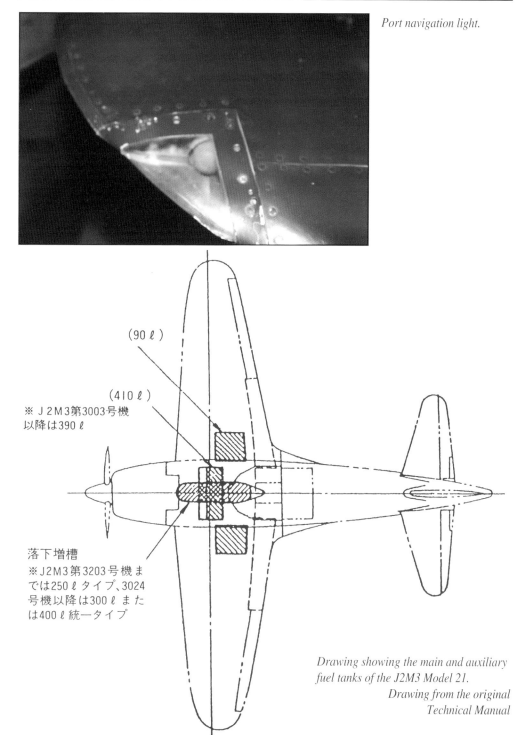

Port navigation light.

(90ℓ)

(410ℓ)

※ J 2 M 3 第 3003 号機
以降は 390ℓ

落下増槽
※ J 2 M 3 第 3203 号機ま
では 250ℓ タイプ、3024
号機以降は 300ℓ また
は 400ℓ 統一タイプ

Drawing showing the main and auxiliary
fuel tanks of the J2M3 Model 21.
Drawing from the original
Technical Manual

Right and below:
Three photos of the aileron
hinge, bottom of the wing.

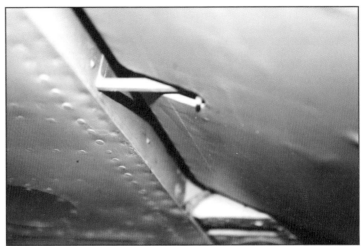

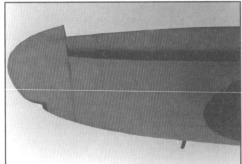

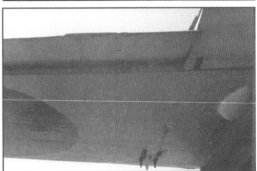

Above:
Two photos of the bottom of the port wing of J2M3.

Right:
Filler cap and the drain tube of 300l drop tank.

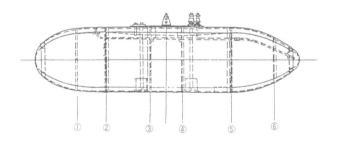

Above:
300 liter fuel drop tank as
was fitted to Raidens.

Right:
300 liter (above) and 400
liter (below) tanks which
were fitted to Raiden.
   *Drawing from Raiden
      Technical Manual.*

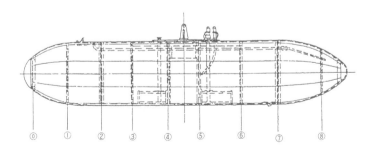

Canopy & Cockpit

Top of the page:
Front view of the port side of the J2M3 canopy.

Above:
Two photos showing canopy details.

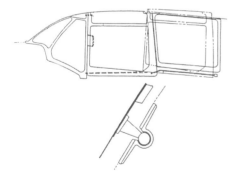

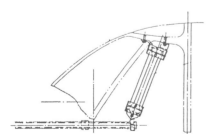

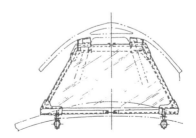

Above:
Starboard side of the wind-
shield. Details of the armour
glass are also visible.

Left:
Drawing of the canopy.
Below:
Details of the armour glass.
Drawings from Technical
Manual.

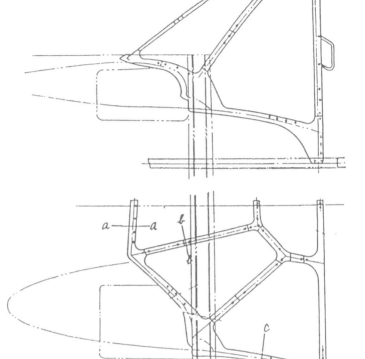

Above:
Canopy from the rear.

Right:
Details of the J2M3 wind-
screen.
Drawing from the Technical
Manual.

Right and below:
Two photos showing details
of the canopy and armoured
glass.

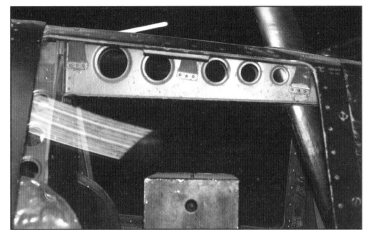

Left:
Details of the rear part of
the canopy and cockpit just
behind the pilot's seat.

Below:
Four photos showing details
of the rear part of the
canopy.

Left:
Movable part of the canopy from the right.

Above:
Wartime photo showing
the pilot's seat and the
headrest.
                via T. Januszewski

Above*: Raiden cockpit just before the restoration. Very simple construction of the control column is also visible.*

Below*: Restored cockpit of the J2M3 but still lacking some of the instruments and details.*

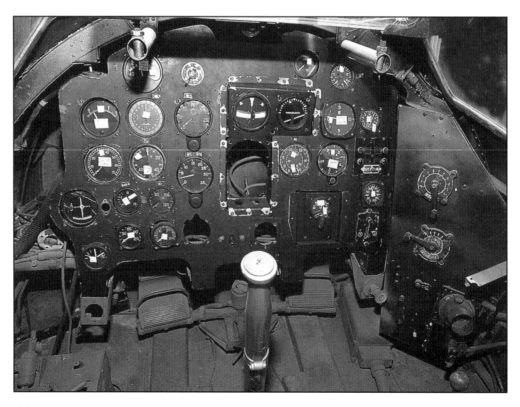

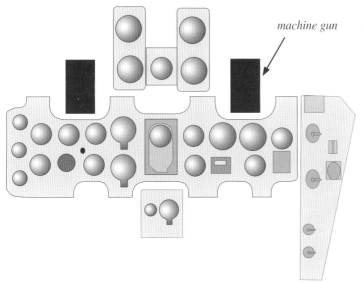

machine gun

*Instrument panel of the
J2M2 Raiden Model 11.*

Not to scale

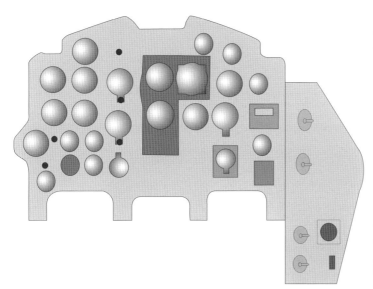

*Instrument panel of the
J2M3 Raiden Model 21.
Very similar if not identical
were panels used on J2M5
and J2M6*

Not to scale

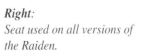

Right:
*Seat used on all versions of
the Raiden.*

Armament

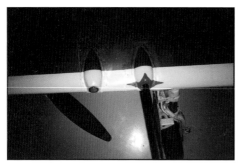

Top of the page:
Armament compartment with panels removed.
20 mm cannons are visible.
Middle of the page (two photos):
Details of the cannons blaste tubes.
Right:
Shell ejection chute of the inboard cannon.

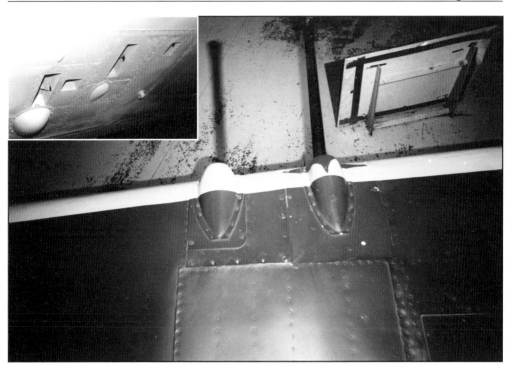

Top, left photo:
Shell ejection chutes, on starboard wing.
Big photo:
Details of the cannons blast tubes from above.
Below:
Drowing of the cannons arragment in the port wing.
Drawing from the Technical Manual.

Details of the inboard cannon.
Drawing from the Technical
Manual.

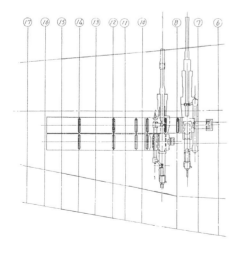

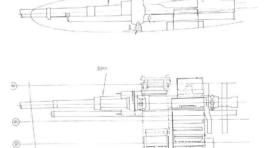

Drawing of the bomb racks used on the Raiden. Drawing from the Technical Manual.

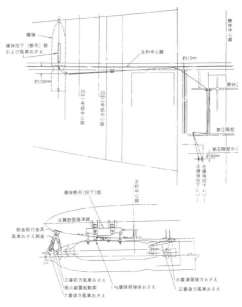

Right photo and bottom left:
Bomb racks under the Raiden's wing.

Bottom, right:
Shell ejection chutes and cannon blister on the port wing.

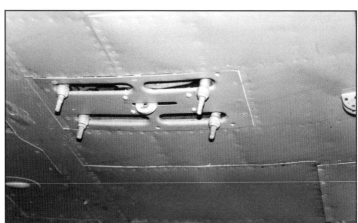

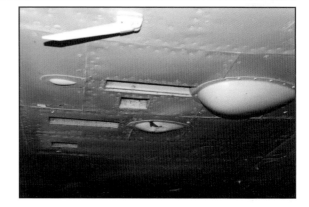

Engine

Above:
J2M3 engine cowling removed. Aircraft before restoration.
Below:
Cowling of the J2M3. Exhaust pipes are also visible.

Above: Mitsubishi Kasei 23ko engine exposed. Oil tank is also visible.
Below: Arrangement of the exhaust pipes of the J2M3. Drawing from the Technical Manual.

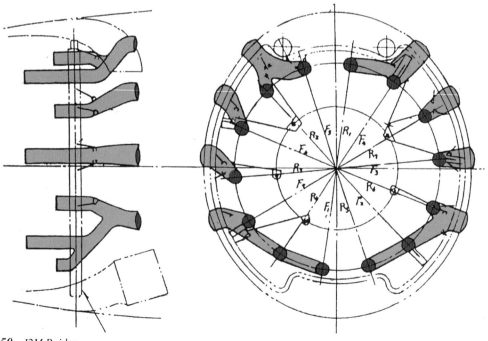

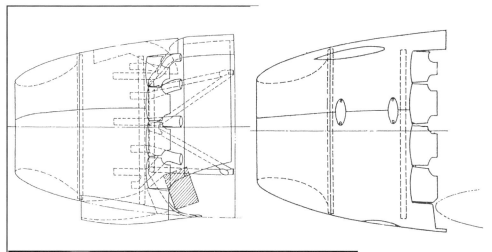

Above:
Cowling of the J2M3
Raiden Model 11 (late)
version.
Drawing from the Technical
Manual.

Left:
Details of the J2M3 cowling
and exhaust pipes.

Below:
Mitsubishi Kasei 23ko
mounts.
Drawing from the Technical
Manual.

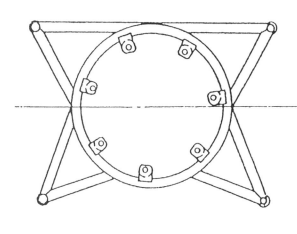

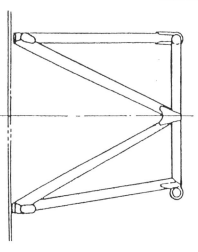

*Mitsubishi Kasei 23ko engine (used on J2M3 and J2M6) found by Americans.
via T. Januszewski*

Details of the cooling fans. Note the shape of the blades.

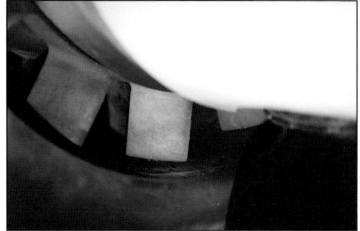

Close up photo of the J2M3 spinner.

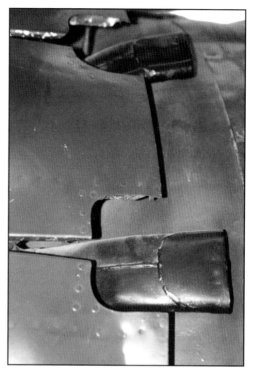

Above and left:
Details of the J2M3 exhaust pipes. Note that pipes
are not rounded but rather flattened.

Below:
Bottom of the Kasei 23ko engine.

Front view of the oil cooler inlet (J2M3).

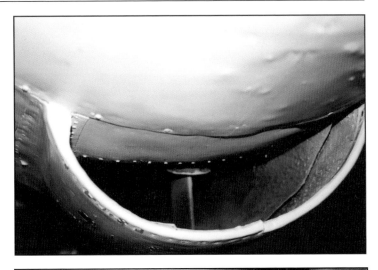

Another shot of the oil cooler, 3/4 bottom view.

Almost plain view othe bottom of the J2M3 oil coller.

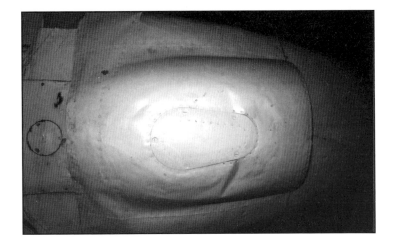

Tail

Above:
Port side of the J2M3 tail.
Right:
Port horizontal stabiliser - bottom.
Below:
Upper side of the port hotizontal stabiliser.

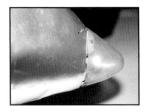

Above:
White navigation light on the rear end of the fuselage.
Right:
Port horizontal stabiliser. Note the details of the panel lines.

Starboard horizontal stabiliser without the elevator. Aircraft before restoration.

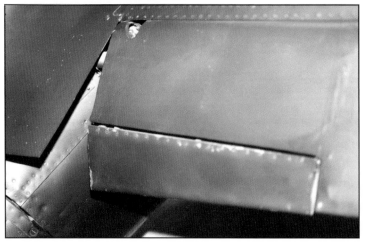

Details of the elevator and trimming tab.

Undercarriage

Above, left:
Port main undercarrige leg cover. Note the shape of the cover.

Above:
Inside view of the port main leg.

Left:
Front view of the starboard main underrciare leg.

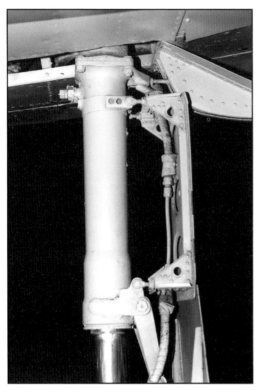
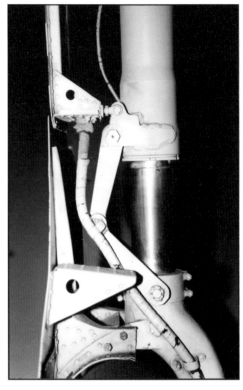

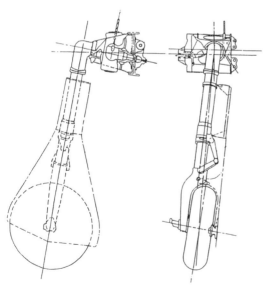

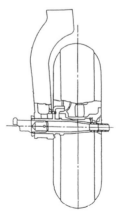

Above, left: *Details of the upper part of the main leg.*
Above: *Close up view of the torque links and brake pipe.*
Left: *Drawing of the main undercarrige from the Technical Manual.*

Two photos of the tail wheel.

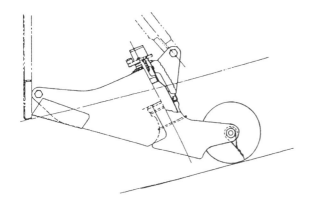

Drawing of the tail wheel arrangement.
Drawing from the Technical Manual.

Upper part of the starboard mail leg cover.

Close up photos of the main wheel well.

Above and left:
Photos of the main wheel well and the inside wheel cover.
Note the shape of the wheel well and internal structure.

Below:
Photo of the upper, separate part of the main leg cover. Note how that cover was moved.

Wartime colour photo of a J2M5 Raiden Model 33. Note the colours of the upper surfaces and the propeller. Aircraft probably of 256 Kókútai. via James F. Lansdale.

Bibliography

Books:

1. Rene Francillon, "Japanese Aircraft of the Pacific War," Putnam, 1979, ISBN 0 370 30251 6, pp. 388-396.
2. Okumiya and Horikoshi with Caidin, "The Zero Fighter," Cassell & Co Ltd, London, 1958, Chapter 4, "The First Naval Interceptor--the Mitsubishi J2M Jack," pp. 209-226, and Appendix A, pp. 269-270.
3. Model Art Company, Issue No. 470, "Japanese Navy Interceptor Fighter Mitsubishi (J2M) Raiden," Tokyo, 1996.
4. Maru Mechanic, Issue No. 43, "Raiden, Shiden, Shiden Kai," Tokyo, 1983, pp. 3-42.
5. Koku-Fan Illustrated Special, Vol. 1, "Japanese Military Aircraft Illustrated: Fighters," Tokyo, 1982, pp. 133-134, 176-185, 270-271.
6. Bunrindo Company, Famous Airplanes of the World, No. 61/1996-11, Navy Interceptor "Raiden," Tokyo, 1996.
7. GAKKEN, Volume No. 29, "Interceptor Fighter Raiden," Tokyo, October 2000.
8. Tadeusz Januszewski, Krzysztof Zalewski, "Japońskie Samoloty Marynarki, 1912-1945", Warszawa, 2000.

Magazines:

1. Aero Technika Lotnicza, Vol 12/92.
2. Revi, Vol. 22, 23
3. Royal Air Force "Flying Review," Vol. XVII, No. 8, May 1962, pp 18-21, article by Michael Farmer entitled "Mitsubishi's Problem Child."
4. Avion No 94 & 95, January and February 2001, article by Michel Ledet and Katsuhiko Osuo "Mitsubishi J2M Raiden".

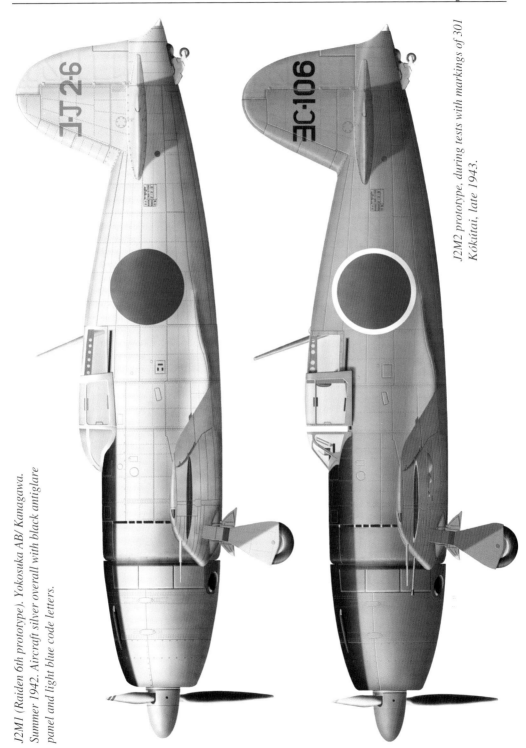

J2M1 (Raiden 6th prototype). Yokosuka AB/ Kanagawa. Summer 1942. Aircraft silver overall with black antiglare panel and light blue code letters.

J2M2 prototype, during tests with markings of 301 Kōkūtai, late 1943.

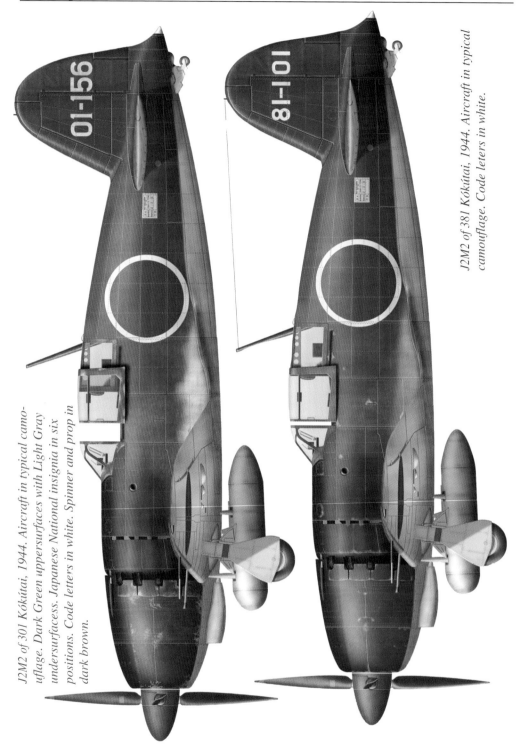

J2M2 of 301 Kōkūtai, 1944. Aircraft in typical camouflage. Dark Green uppersurfaces with Light Gray undersurfacess. Japanese National insignia in six positions. Code leters in white. Spinner and prop in dark brown.

J2M2 of 381 Kōkūtai, 1944. Aircraft in typical camouflage. Code leters in white.

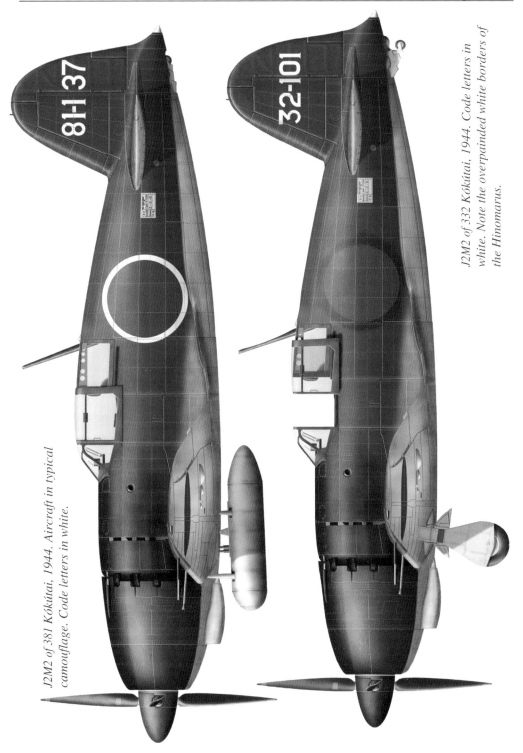

J2M2 of 381 Kōkūtai, 1944. Aircraft in typical camouflage. Code letters in white.

J2M2 of 332 Kōkūtai, 1944. Code letters in white. Note the overpainded white borders of the Hinomarus.

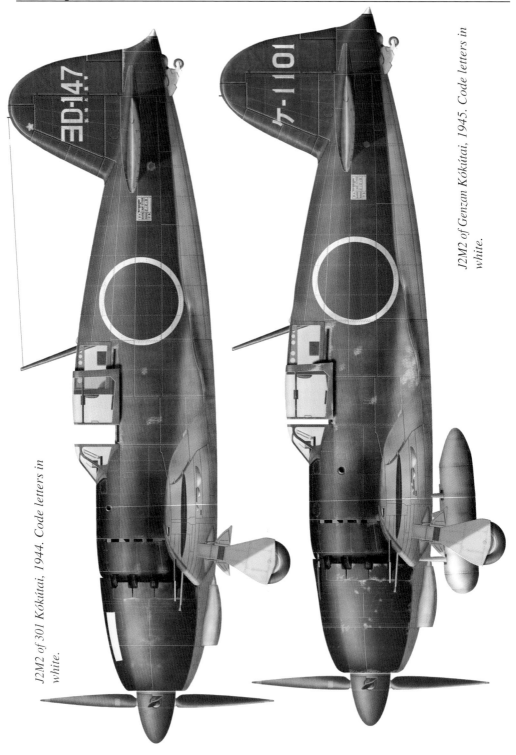

J2M2 of Genzan Kōkūtai, 1945. Code letters in white.

J2M2 of 301 Kōkūtai, 1944. Code letters in white.

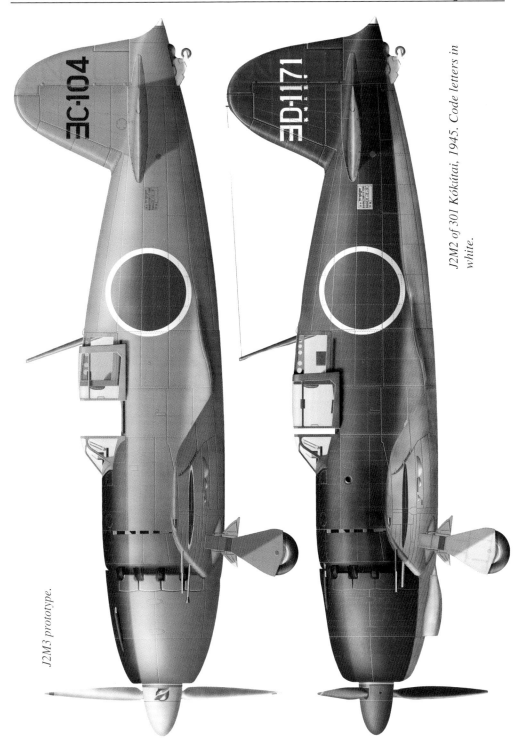

J2M3 prototype.

J2M2 of 301 Kōkūtai, 1945. Code letters in white.

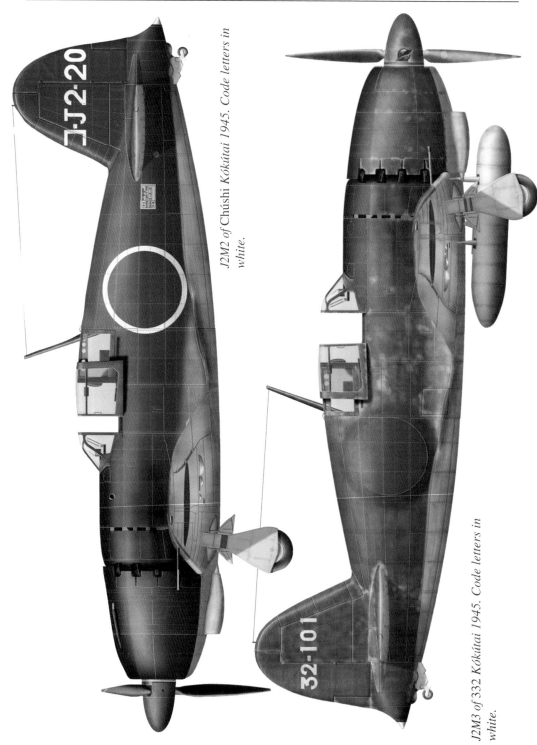

J2M2 of Chūshi *Kōkūtai 1945. Code letters in white.*

J2M3 of 332 Kōkūtai 1945. Code letters in white.

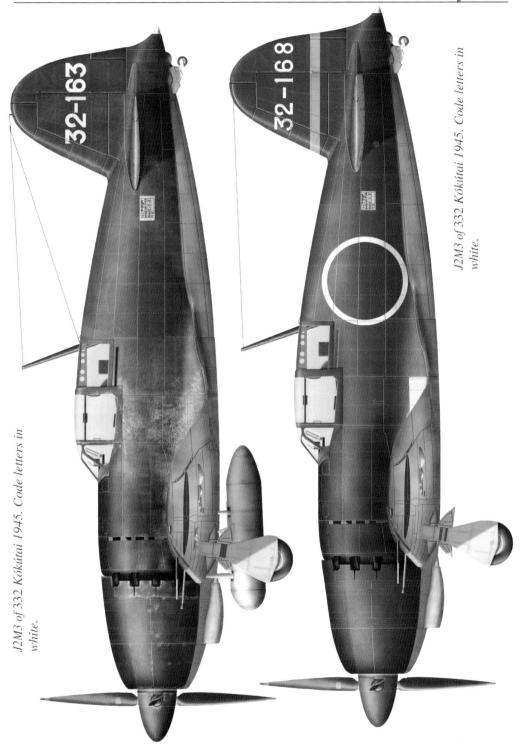

J2M3 of 332 Kōkūtai 1945. Code letters in white.

J2M3 of 332 Kōkūtai 1945. Code letters in white.

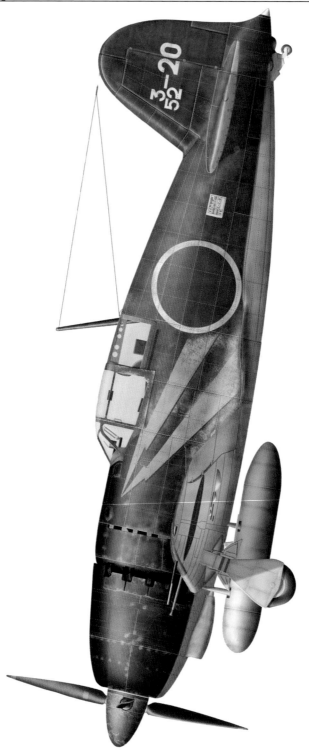

J2M3 of 352 Kōkūtai 1945. Code letters in white.

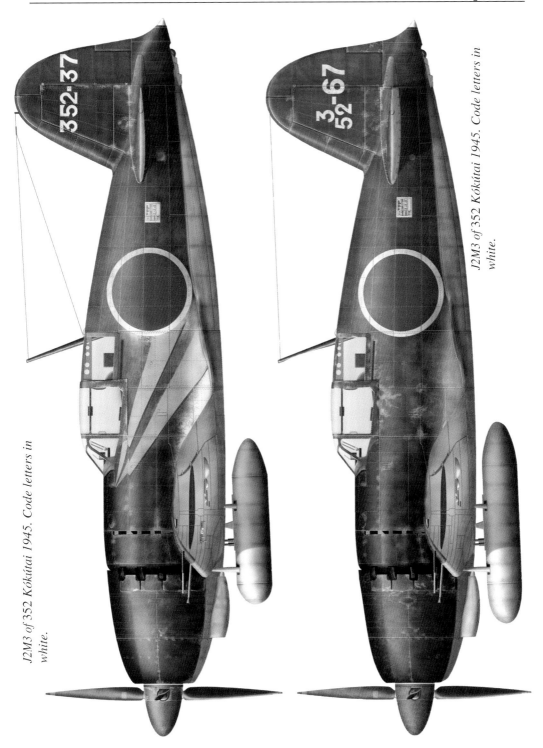

J2M3 of 352 Kōkūtai 1945. Code letters in white.

J2M3 of 352 Kōkūtai 1945. Code letters in white.

J2M3 tested by the British. Aircraft in typical Japanese camouflage with British roundels

J2M3 of 302 Kōkūtai 1945. Code letters in white.

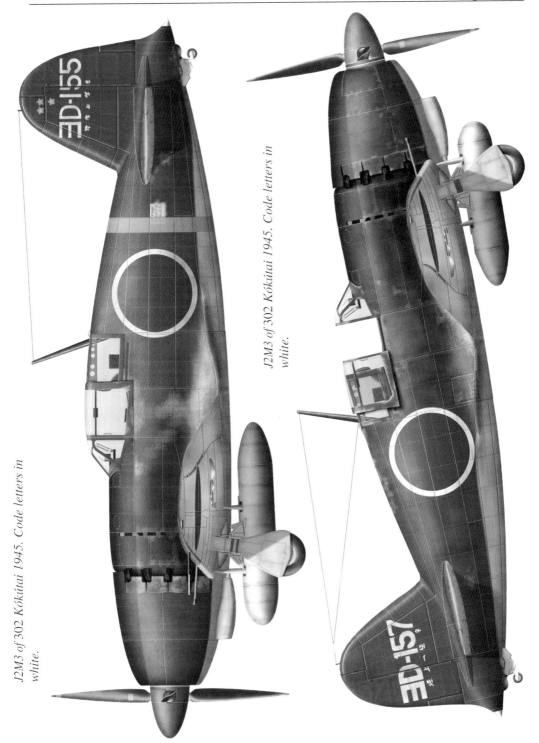

J2M3 of 302 Kōkūtai 1945. Code letters in white.

J2M3 of 302 Kōkūtai 1945. Code letters in white.

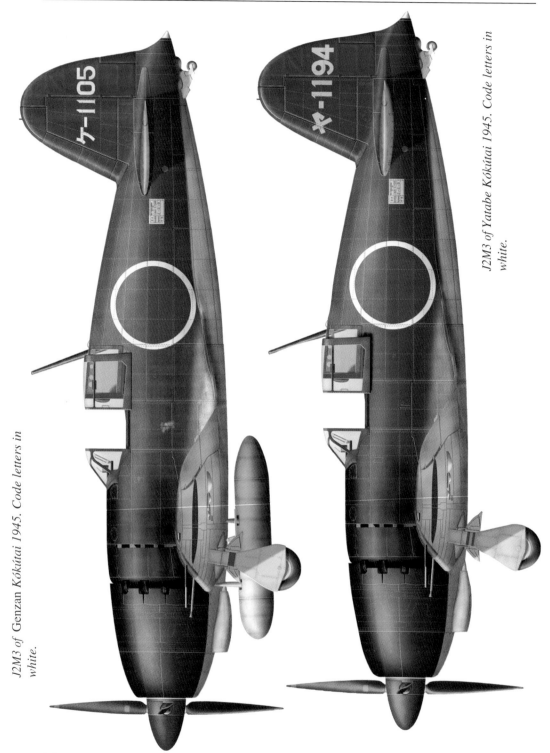

J2M3 of Genzan Kōkūtai 1945. Code letters in white.

J2M3 of Yatabe Kōkūtai 1945. Code letters in white.

J2M3 of 302 Kókútai 1945. Code letters in white.

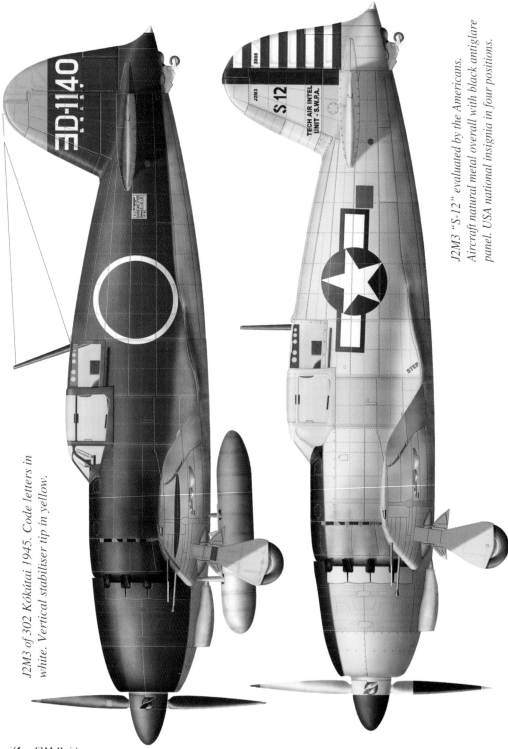

J2M3 of 302 Kōkūtai 1945. Code letters in white. Vertical stabiliser tip in yellow.

J2M3 "S-12" evaluated by the Americans. Aircraft natural metal overall with black antiglare panel. USA national insignia in four positions.

J2M3 of Tainan Kókútai *1945. Code letters in white.*

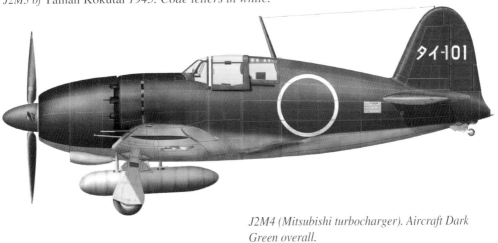

J2M4 (Mitsubishi turbocharger). Aircraft Dark Green overall.

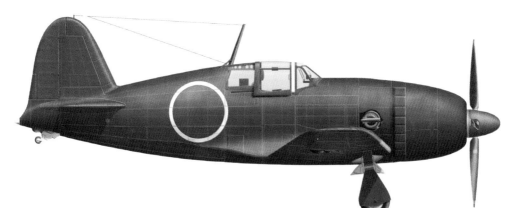

J2M5 of 256 Kókútai 1945. Code letters in yellow.

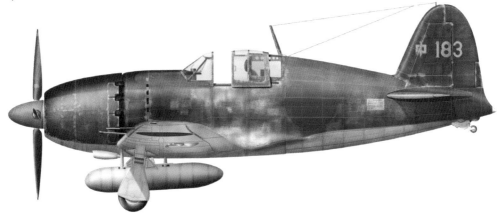

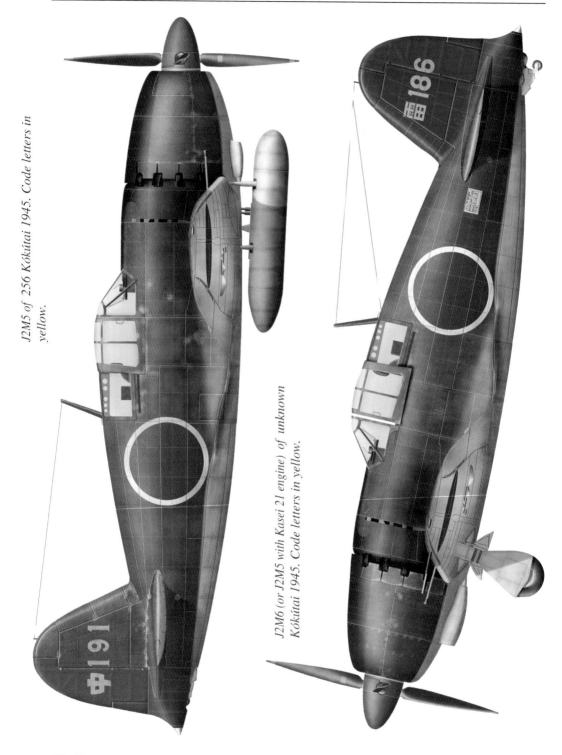

J2M5 of 256 Kōkūtai 1945. Code letters in yellow.

J2M6 (or J2M5 with Kasei 21 engine) of unknown Kōkūtai 1945. Code letters in yellow.

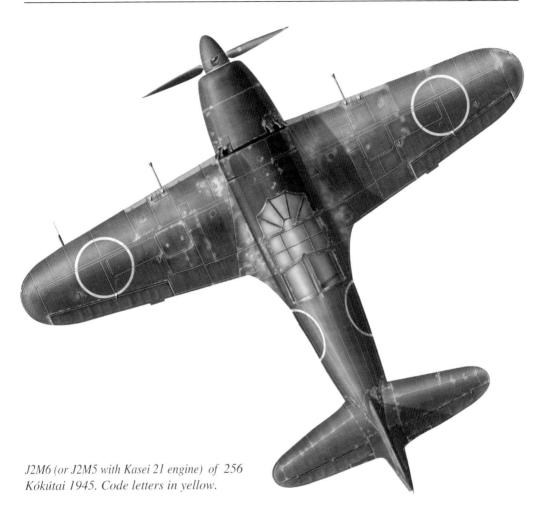

J2M6 (or J2M5 with Kasei 21 engine) of 256 Kókútai 1945. Code letters in yellow.

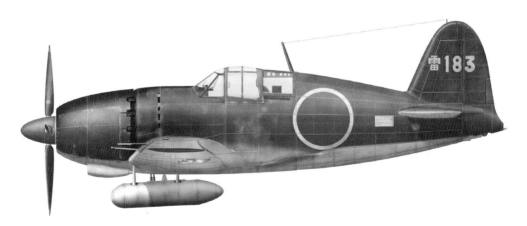

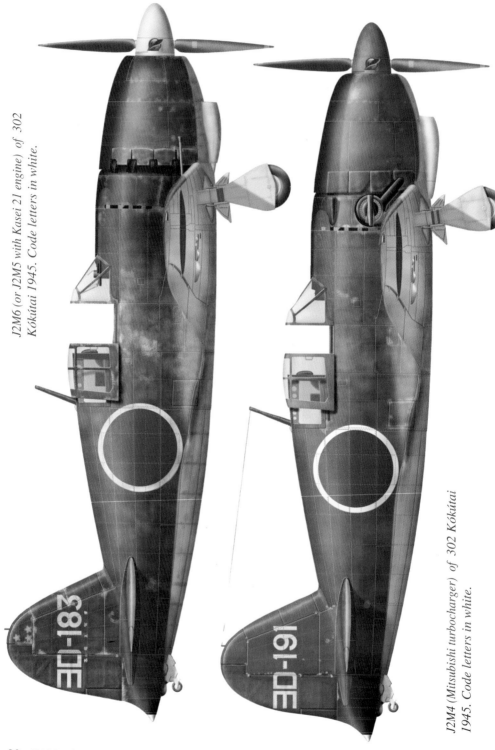

J2M6 (or J2M5 with Kasei 21 engine) of 302 Kōkūtai 1945. Code letters in white.

J2M4 (Mitsubishi turbocharger) of 302 Kōkūtai 1945. Code letters in white.